the fantastic hairdresser

Alan Austin-Smith

Fantastic Hairdresser Company Ltd, London

This book is dedicated to Irene Field

Fantastic Hairdresser Company Ltd
Barley Mow Centre,
10 Barley Mow Passage,
Chiswick, W4 4PH

First published in 2003

Editor: Carolyn Field
Design & creative: **bluw**□□□
Printed by Steffprint

A catalogue record of this book is available from the British Library

ISBN No.0-9546083

Printed in UK

Acknowledgements

This book is the culmination of over 25 years of working alongside Fantastic Hairdressers, thanks to all of you — a part of you is in everything I teach.

The rest of this page is a thank you to the people who have influenced my life in so many ways, there is not enough room for all of you, but here we go:

Mum and Dad, I know you are always guiding me. Christine I hope you are proud of your little (big!) brother. Gary, thanks for so many laughs, you're a great friend, and Tim, you are always looking after me — a real friend. The Fields' (and the Stoneham!) — you really are the most wonderful people, thank you for your love. Tony, your love for Irene and your family has been the biggest inspiration in my life.

So many at Vidal Sassoon's — Bond St, 1976-1980 (I was Dale!) but a special thanks to Nigel Sillis, my first manager, and Anthony, Oliver and Paul for introducing me to beautiful hair. Jane, Veronica, Christine, Debbie, and everyone else at Fenwicks — I have such good memories from those days. Graham and Barbara, thanks for helping me to believe in me!

At L'Oreal, again too many - Paul Timberlake, you taught me how to entertain an audience. Brian, thanks for making me commercial, and supporting me in my crazy schemes. Suzanne and Janine, great friends, great times, thanks. My brilliant team — thanks for letting me learn how to be a manager with you.

Catrina, I'm so proud of you, Mike, your fantastic book inspired me to do this one, the Success Scholars, I only hope that you got as much from me as I got from you — great friends for ever, thank you. All our customers — thank you for your support over the years, it means so much to us

Chris, thanks for re-igniting the ambition, and Alex, you are the most creative person I know — believe in yourself.

And finally — the five most important people in my life — without you- it would all be for nothing — you are everything to me. Anny — I love you more than there are stars in the sky, you always inspire and delight me. Craig and Sam, you bring so much joy to my life, I am so proud of you — you are both such special people. Nathan, it makes me so happy to see you happy, you have a wonderful future, and thanks for those great big huggles!

And finally Carolyn - My business partner, my friend, the mother of two of my children, and my ex wife! Carolyn this book is yours as much as it is mine; it's the result of everything we have achieved together over the last 15 years. Thank you for your support and your unfailing belief in me.

I know this is too long — but I don't care — it's my book!!

introduction
how to use this book

6. the fantastic hairdresser is an ambassador
understands it's a business
has high values
needs help

7. the fantastic hairdresser is a performer
uses DOGASHI
changes their mind
is an actor

8. the fantastic hairdresser is alive inside
knows where they are going
has no limits
makes movies

9. the fantastic hairdresser is always learning
understands that excellence is a journey
knows how they learn
minds their own business

and finally... the fantastic hairdresser has fun

contact details on courses with take control
about the author

introduction

Why did I write this book? I guess it's the same reason I still work in the hairdressing industry.

I am constantly being asked why I still work in this industry. As you may know, I started my career as a hairdresser before I joined L'Oreal and began to understand hairdressing in a different way. I began to understand the potential we had as hairdressers, to realise what an amazing business it is, but perhaps most importantly of all - to see clearly why we are not achieving that potential.

To see why, at that time, we were losing business and were not attracting quality people to the job.

With dreadful service, cheap prices, poor wages & working conditions, out of date management, and non-existent profit, I don't think it is an exaggeration to say that the industry was nearly bankrupt.

In fact if it wasn't for the fact that people have to get their haircut, then I think it quite easily could have been.

It has been fantastic to see these things change over the last 15 years, and obviously very satisfying to know that I, along with many others, have had something to with those changes. As my company has developed over that time, I have become involved with other industries and business sectors, which broadens my knowledge and understanding, enhancing what I bring to the table when I am consulting or coaching in hairdressing.

However it is this that brings some people to question "Why are you still working in the hairdressing industry?"

This question comes from those who still have a view of hairdressing based on the past. People are amazed when I tell them about an industry that is worth £3.8 billion a year in the UK alone, and about salons that turnover in excess of £500,000 from one unit with stylists that can earn over £500 per week (if you just read that and thought well I'm not, then please carry on reading because this book will show you how to). It also comes from people within the industry who seem to think that the improvements we have made over the last 15 years are enough - there is nothing more to do.

It's this point that probably concerns me the most.

"Excellence is a journey" is something you will read about in the following pages. You can't stop learning, changing and growing in today's world. It moves too quickly. Just stop and look at the speed the world changes at today. Any hesitation and you are left behind. So that's why I still work in this industry. Firstly I love it, it's fun, creative and full of great people. Secondly there is still a job to do for my industry to achieve the potential it has. We aren't finished yet, not by a long way.

This finally brings me to "Why this book?"

It's because I feel the next step we need to take, is to stretch ourselves even further. To move beyond being good hairdressers and become fantastic hairdressers.

As stylists we need to get out of the comfort zone and reach for the stars!

As trainees we need to set our sights higher on what we want to achieve, and as managers and coaches, we have to be clear of what we are motivating people towards.

Which is simply, to become a "Fantastic Hairdresser"

how to use this book

I have tried to make this book as flexible as possible. You can read it cover to cover if that is how you want to, or you can read specific sections that you feel are relevant to you.

Alternatively you can randomly open the pages and read where you fall, and I guarantee you will always find something relevant to you.

Of course it's up to you how you use this book, but please, please, use it.

If you have any ambition for yourself and for your industry then make a commitment now to taking the first steps on the journey from good hairdresser to fantastic hairdresser.

If you are going to read it cover to cover, then I suggest that you break it into small chunks. If you read this book in one sitting, then you will not give yourself the time needed to reflect on what you have learnt, and how it will affect you.

Why not try reading one chapter per day for the next ten days.

Give yourself weekends off, which gives you two weeks worth of reading in short chunks and reflection to enable you to take the action that will make a difference.

However, if you do decide to use this book randomly, I would strongly suggest that you do still read the first 2 chapters. These introduce some core concepts that will give you the foundations of success and make everything else more relevant. After that you can do as you wish.

You will find some sections of the book have spaces to write in, or simple exercises for you to do, as well as the ACTION pages at the end of each chapter.

Please use these. Write in this book. Make it yours. Jot your thoughts and comments in the margin.

This is not just a book, it's an opportunity for you to make a difference,

and as such you will probably want to go back to certain sections and review them. You will also probably use it to coach others; to help others stretch themselves and realise their potential. So add to this book. Add your own opinions, ideas and things you want to change. In fact start right now and put your name in the front. Make it yours!

I love the fact that eventually each book out there becomes individual, unique, different to the next one, because of the views and pointers that you have added to it.

Finally please recognise that although this book is about being a fantastic hairdresser, it won't take you long to realise that it is much more than that. The principles in this book can be applied to any job, or any part of your life. Be creative, look outside the box, and the fantastic hairdresser will help you in all areas of your life.

You don't have to be a hairdresser to get something special from this book!

1

SUCCESS

WHAT IS IT?

Look at a clock, or a watch - or if you can't find either, just count it. But I want you to remind yourself how long a second is. 1.....2. That's it, just one second. The difference between first and last place in the Olympic 100 metres final will be less than that - less than one second. The difference between first and second, will be measured in hundredths of a second. Take that second again - 1.....2, and now break it down into hundredths and think about what one or two hundredths of a second is. You can't? Of course you can't. It is impossible to imagine, but that can be the difference between success and failure.

What am I saying here? Simply, that if the only difference between those 8 athletes is less than 1 second, then they all have the technique, power and ability to run as fast as each other. So how come one or two of them will consistently win every time?

I have always been fascinated by successful people. What is it that makes the difference? Essentially we all have the same opportunities. You may kid yourself that you are a special case, but there are countless stories of people from disadvantaged backgrounds or who are not fully able in some way, that have achieved exceptional levels of success.

If a 2 year old had the same levels of perseverance and patience as an adult, wouldn't we still be crawling around on all fours? Think about it. Learning to walk takes real commitment. But look at how easily we as adults give up on things, how we believe that we can't change, or don't have the discipline or patience to stick at it. With that sort of attitude as a two year old, we would never have bothered to progress from crawling!

So what is the difference? Successful people aren't more intelligent, they don't have bigger brains, they don't start with more money - it is all about the other stuff!

THE OTHER STUFF ←

Why does one athlete consistently win the 100 metres? Why does one footballer score more goals than another, a waitress get more tips, or a sales person hit more targets? What makes fantastic hairdressers like Trevor Sorbie, Anthony Mascolo, Charles Worthington different?

Not just the big names either - you have fantastic hairdressers working with you - they consistently produce good work, send clients out the door feeling fantastic, earn high wages and make good tips. It doesn't matter what you look at,

50% of what makes you good at what you do, is what I call the other stuff.

All tennis players know how to play tennis, and all the top ones know how to play it well, so what is the difference that makes champions? The other stuff! The 50% that is about attitude, confidence, motivation, drive, etc.

There are so many things we can learn from the people who are achieving great things. The first is that truly successful people are having a great time; they enjoy what they do. Success in hairdressing isn't just about being one of those names I mentioned above - that may not be what you want - but ultimately it's about being happy with what you are doing. Surely you want to enjoy what you do.

▶ WHAT IS SUCCESS?

This question is asked over and over again. I believe it is often the cause of a lot of frustration and dissatisfaction for people, as sometimes they are chasing something that isn't necessarily what they want.

One of my favourite quotes is "Excellence is a journey, not a destination".

Everybody wants to be successful, excellent at what they do don't they? Well interestingly some people tell me that they don't. It took me a while to work this out, before I realised that all it was, the only difference, was people's perception of success. The people who say that they don't want to be successful, are basing their understanding of success on what we are fed by the media etc: money, cars, big promotions and so on.

Of course to some people this is success, but to others, success is about being a good parent, a fun friend, enjoying their job, regardless of how much money they have, or how big their house is. So who is right? They both are, because success is simply achieving what you want to achieve and then enjoying it.

It is your life after all, and as long as what you want is ethical, moral and legal, who am I or anyone else for that matter, to judge you?

modelling

model successful people

Working from this premise, then the first thing you have to do - is decide what success is to you?

The exercise at the end of this chapter will help you here, as I find the best way to do this, is to find the people that you perceive as successful and think about why you have chosen them.

This will give you a good insight into what you regard as success. Remember - don't just choose famous people - when you broaden the parameters of success ,

there are lots of 'normal' people achieving success in their lives, that you can learn from.

The next step is to look closely at those people who are achieving the sort of success that you want, operating the way you want to, and learn from them.

Watch successful people and learn their secrets - trust me - they are not doing anything that you can't do.

Look at the people in your salon who are achieving results - what are they doing differently to you? Go to as many shows and presentations as you can and learn from the greats. Listen to them, but listen from a position of knowledge that they are not special people - just normal people who are doing something you aren't.

Do you want more of your clients to have colour but find it difficult? Then find a person in your salon who has more colour clients and listen to them talk to their customers. If you are training to be a hairdresser, then make sure you listen to consultations. This is the key to a fantastic hairdresser, and it's there for you to learn - if you can be bothered. Unfortunately, too often this time is seen as an opportunity to dive into the staff room before you are asked to shampoo! (Been there!)

➡ **Do you want to live in a nice house one day?**

➡ **Drive a lovely car?**

➡ **Wear great clothes and have fantastic holidays?**

➡ **Do you want to be happy, satisfied, and proud of what you do - to have the respect of your colleagues and for people in your life to be proud of you?**

Then make the decision, NOW, to be fantastic at what you do, not just good at it. Learn from those who are doing it already. It's all there, right in front of you, you just have to open your eyes and ears and take it in!

Write down the people you are going to learn from and how you are going to do it. If they are famous personalities, or hairdressing icons, then look out for interviews with them, or read their biographies. They may be colleagues, family or friends. Start to watch, learn and listen for what they are doing differently.

Successful people I will learn from:

millions of moments

Let's take this a stage further. We are talking about success, and I guess we all want to have a successful life.

Do you want to be eternally happy? Be successful in your life? Well let me show you how.

WHAT IS LIFE? ⟵

The problem is that a lot of people don't really understand what 'life' is. So how can you have a successful one, if you don't even know?

To be happy in your life, you have to understand what life is.

Let me ask you a couple of strange questions. Can I kill you now, right now this moment - yesterday? Can I kill you now, right now - tomorrow? Of course not. You are not alive yet tomorrow, so how can I kill you? Interestingly, you are not alive yesterday anymore either. So when can I kill you? NOW, is the answer. The only time I could take your life, is now. Because it's the only moment it is there to be taken!

You may not of thought about it like this before, but there is only one moment you are alive - when your heart is beating, your mind is thinking, your body is breathing - and that is NOW.

So what is life? It's now - it is happening right now as you read this book.

We need to stop looking at life as a whole - a 70 to 80 year long experience. Life is made up of millions of moments.

Every life is made up of so many years, each year is made up of 365 days and every day is filled with many moments.

A moment of love, fun, energy, achievement, excitement, satisfaction, or simply the accomplishment of some task in your work or life.

I know what some of you are thinking though;

"What about the crappy moments?" "The moments of despair, disappointment, lost love, anger, tiredness, boredom and failure".

Well I'll come to those in a moment, but for now let's just work on the premise that they are all moments, whether they are good or bad.

THE PAST AND THE FUTURE

Life is made up of millions of moments and the only control you have in your life is in the current one.

Think about it; what can you do about the past?

One thing - learn from it. Learn how to have a good time - you have good pasts and you can learn not to have a bad time from the not so good ones. But that is it!

Once you have learnt the lessons, there is nothing else you can do about the past. You can't change it, it's happened. Makes you wonder why we spend so much time beating ourselves up for the mistakes we have made in the past. Once you have learned from them -that's it, there is nothing you can do to change them.

What about the future, what can we do about that?

Plan for it, prepare for it, but that's all - you don't even know if it's going to happen.

What do personal, or world disasters teach us? What does a near miss in the car teach us, or a health scare? That life is fragile; none of us have a clue what is going to happen in the next ten minutes, let alone 5 years.

How many plans have changed in your life? Some for the better some for the worse, but I bet there are plenty. Now think about how much time and energy we waste worrying about what might happen in the future - a future that we have no control over at all. Crazy isn't it.

worry
is the misuse of
imagination

take control

It's the name of our company, and this is why.

I think we all understand that to be happy in life, to be successful, we have to take control.

This can seem like such a huge task, but it's not, when you recognise that all you have to do (or more importantly, are able to) is take control of the present moment, the now - what is happening right now.

So what about those crappy moments? Well, they will always be there;

we are human beings, with emotions and issues to deal with, but what we have to realise is that these are just moments - moments that can pass, become history that we can learn from, and that is all!

The more we understand this, the easier it is to move past the genuinely bad times. But also to change the way we are operating or thinking at those times and turn some of the crappy moments in to better ones.

So a successful life is actually a life filled with lots of little successes.

There it is - the first secret of a Fantastic Hairdresser or a fantastic anything for that matter.

Take Control - the way you deal with each moment in your life, determines how successful it is. The more successful, happy moments you have, the happier and more successful you will be.

On our seminars, we do an exercise, which is one of my favourites.

I ask the audience to think of 3 successful moments in their life and write them on a post it note, which they then stick on the wall.

Remember it's what is successful for you.

It does not have to be some huge world changing success - it could simply be passing your driving test, or receiving praise for something you have done at school, home or work. I can still remember vividly, scoring the winning goal in the cup final when I was 8!

Then I ask the audience to do the same with happy moments. Really good memories. Of course we get lots of weddings and births, but some of them are really different - ranging from swimming with dolphins through to laughing with a friend. Some of them are also far too rude for me to put in here, but I'm sure you can use your imagination!

It's fantastic! All those people thinking of happy and successful moments from their past, writing them down and sticking them proudly on the wall. I then ask them to do it again - think of another three, and again. The interesting thing is, it starts to get easier as you get into the groove of thinking about those things. It makes you realise that we don't spend enough time recognising the good stuff that has happened in our life, sometimes focusing too much on the crappy stuff. Try it for yourself, fill in the 'post-it' notes below and see how nice it feels.

3 happy moments

3 successful moments

3 more happy moments

3 more successful moments

and another
3 happy moments!

and another
3 successful moments!

TLC - the Total Life Concept

I've always believed that you must have some idea of the direction you are heading in life, but even more importantly, and something that is often missed is that you have to know where you are starting from.

The Total Life Concept helps you identify where you are at the moment, and more importantly, where you should be.

This wonderful tool started life as the Total Product Concept, a marketing tool that I learnt from Tom Peters. However, the more I used it, the more I realised that it wasn't just about marketing, or even business. It was about everything. That's when I named it TLC - the Total Life Concept.

It starts at the centre with the 'core' of what you do. For example the 'core' reason a hairdressing salon exists is to cut peoples hair. A hotel is there because people need a bed and restaurants are for eating in.

EXPECTED

Then it moves out to the next ring, with 'expected'.

I go to your salon for a haircut, but I expect a certain level of service. I expect to be able to have colour on my hair if I want, to have a coffee, to be offered a magazine etc.

How many people do you know that stop here in their life. They do what is expected - but no more. The person who finishes work on the dot, regardless of what needs to be done. The stylist who doesn't think they need to learn anymore, or who doesn't think it's their job to help keep the salon clean, has stopped in 'expected'.

I was discussing business training with a salon owner who came out with a line I will always remember. He didn't see that he needed any training, as in his own words:

"We are no worse than anyone else in this town!"

Isn't that amazing? I am a very visual person and I already had a whole marketing campaign going on in my mind - posters at key sites, banners in the window, newspaper adverts all carrying the line "Come to us, we are no worse than anyone else!"

If anything sums up people stopping at "expected" then that line is it.

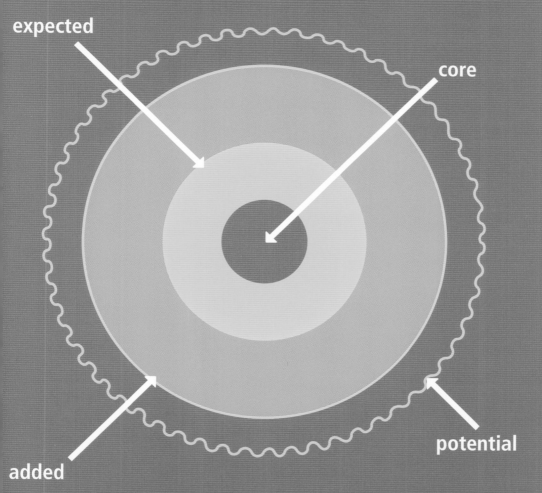

ADDED

The next ring is the 'added' part of the model. Going further than expected, taking that extra step, exceeding the expectations. We all know what this feels like when it happens to us. It's great.

"I expected a certain level of service - but wow, I didn't expect this!"

When any individual or company goes beyond expectations, they create a fantastic response.

I know a beauty therapist who sends thank you cards to all her new clients - It is not the company policy, she does it off her own back!

Interestingly when I discovered this person, she was working in a new salon, having started 6 months earlier with three other therapists. After 6 months, one of the four is consistently fully booked, whilst the other three sit around moaning that there are not enough clients. No prizes for guessing which one is fully booked!

Is this where the winners are? Well it certainly looks like it. But actually it's not. In fact if you are sitting in 'added', patting yourself on the back for all the great things that you do - you are actually in 'expected', and you probably don't even realise it.

POTENTIAL

It is this final part of the Total Life Concept where you find the winners 'Potential'. It's here where you ask: "What's next? Now what do I do?"

It's here where the key to survival is, in this ever changing world - Creativity.

As I have just said, many people are sitting around in 'added' feeling good about themselves because of what they do and how they do it. Not realising that what was once special - the service you provide, the way you deal with your clients, the hair work that you do, has now become the norm - expected.

The only way to stay ahead is to be constantly in 'potential'. Always moving, growing and learning - creatively looking for what's next.

the story of a kettle

You see, the model works from the outside in - A hotel somewhere, whilst in 'potential' (the outside) - decided to put kettles in all their rooms. The moment they did this, the kettle moved into the "added" part of the model, with you the guest pleasantly surprised to find a kettle in your room.

But now, if you checked into a hotel tonight - you would "expect" a kettle in your room.

So the kettle in a hotel room started it's life in 'potential', moved into 'added', and finished up in 'expected'.

THIS HAPPENS TO EVERYTHING! ◄

Think about it and you will see I'm right. Everything starts with a creative idea, spends a period of time being unique, different, special, before eventually becoming the norm and ending up as expected. If you are not in 'potential', you are in 'expected' - standing still, in the one place you can't afford to if you want to be successful today.

Finally think about why I changed the name to total LIFE concept. Look at relationships and see how that early excitement of 'potential' turns into a wonderful time of your life in 'added' but can become so boring and flat in 'expected'.

This model applies to all areas of your life - you have to spend as much time as you can in the outer circle to stay ahead of the game, to achieve the success that you want in each moment.

"Excellence is a journey — not a destination"

The more successful moments you have — the more successful you are

choose 3 goals from this chapter that you can take immediate action on:

2

Learn from

Successful People

the success pyramid

This is a model that I created after spending many years 'modelling' - studying successful people in all walks of life. Identifying with the people that I consider to be successful, looking at what it was that they were doing, and then pulling together the common characteristics that they all shared.

Success is at the peak of the pyramid, which is obviously where we are going, but I want to start in the centre with 'learn'.

The first lesson I discovered is simply that you can't learn to be successful.

Everybody is doing it - reading books, magazines, going on courses, surfing the internet. So many people are committed to learning today, but I fear that many people in their last moments of this life will be saying "I did all that learning but nothing ever happened for me. Nothing changed."

You can't learn to be successful. What am I doing, talking myself out of business? Am I saying you should shut this book now and forget about it? Of course not. All I'm saying is that learning on its own will not take you to success. You need to fill in the box above it with - action.

The population can quite easily split in to those who are taking the action they need to and those who are waiting for it to happen to them.

Have you ever read a book, or attended a course and learnt something that you knew was critical to you? That made you think - "That's me! I must do something about that" and then.... taken no action. Well I've got my hand up here, have you? It is the action that you take with what you learn that will get you to success, not just learning on it's own. Sometimes when I'm running a course, people ask me what time will we be finishing. I always say around 5 o'clock, but what I should really say is, well I'm finishing at about 5, but you're just starting.

Learning isn't the last step, it's the first step.

So what about the other two slices of the pyramid? At the bottom is responsibility, and then above it, discipline.

It all starts with responsibility - everything does

Anything that anybody has ever achieved has only happened when they took responsibility first. However, having taken responsibility to make a change in your life, you now need the discipline to keep it going.

Have you ever taken responsibility for your health or wealth? You know - it's when you decide to smoke less, drink less, exercise more, save more money etc. I'm sure you are already ahead of me here - it's one thing to take responsibility to start those things; it's another to have the discipline to keep it going.

This is how the pyramid works. First you take responsibility for the action you need to take. Then you have to have the discipline to keep doing it. Finally, learn more about the action you have to take, in order to reach the peak of the pyramid.

Over the next few pages I want to go through some of the sections of the pyramid in more detail. I believe that if you are going to get the most out of this book, then you have to apply the principles of the Success Pyramid to your life.

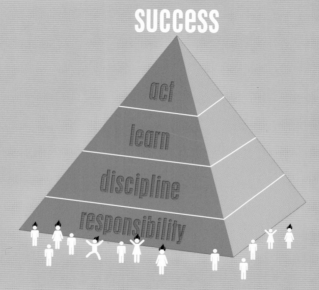

As I've just mentioned, learning on its own won't achieve anything. It's the action that you take with what you learn that makes the difference.

The millionaire hairdresser

A hairdresser I know, was 21 when she learnt a tool from me called the 10% rule. Simply, it means saving 10% of your salary to invest in your future.

She was earning around £150 per week at the time, so was putting £15 a week away. She also decided to add half her tips to that as well which was another £15 a week. This gave her a total of £120 per month, giving her £1,440 per year.

She then realised that if she could increase her average bill by £5 that meant she could add as much as £50 to her wages, which gave her another £5 a week - £20 per month - £240 per year giving her £1,680 that year.

The next year she decided to put 20% away. She was now earning £250 per week with about £40 a week in tips. The 20% added to half her tips gave her £70 a week to put away - £3,360 by the end of the year.

She now had £5,040 saved! She used this as a deposit on a small flat for herself worth £50,000. That was ten years ago. The flat is now worth £150,000 and she only has 15 years left on the mortgage.

Here is the really interesting bit though - she carried on putting her 20% aside. Her salary grew, as did her tips, as she began to understand the true concept of a fantastic hairdresser and delighting her customers. Two years later she bought another flat, which she rented out, whilst living in her original flat.

She has just purchased her 5th property - having bought one every 2 years for the last 10 years.

She is now a 31 year old stylist - she decided she didn't want her own salon, or even any management responsibility. She loves her job - making people look and feel fantastic.

She also has a property portfolio currently worth over £1,200,000.

This is a hairdresser - not a salon owner, not an industry icon - just a normal stylist who did something special.

However, even though it was special, it was something that anyone can do;

she simply took action on something that she had learnt.

That's it - that's all she did. But to do it, she needed the other parts of the pyramid - responsibility and discipline.

Firstly she had to take responsibility, to listen to me, as I hope you are now, and think "that's me, I need to get more control over my money. I can earn what I want, I can have what I want - it's up to me". Then she had to have the discipline to keep it going, to stay focused on why she was doing what she was doing.

Interestingly, she will tell you that eventually this became easy, because it became a habit, a part of her life. So discipline was not a problem any more.

If you want change, change something

Responsibility - if it's to be, it's up to me:

Firstly it is important that you understand the difference between responsibility, and blame or fault. Of course sometimes you are taking responsibility for the blame - "it was my fault". But there is a difference between the two.

Many people say to me that their boss doesn't respect them, doesn't communicate well, or doesn't have any time for them. Or I hear that their partner in life doesn't give them the love and affection that they would like.

Often these people are saying "it's not my fault", and maybe it isn't, but my question is always the same - do you want it to change? And if the answer is yes, then it is your responsibility to do something about it, even if it's not your fault.

"If you want change, change something"

The fly test:

We all need to do the fly test in certain areas of our life. What is a fly test?

Picture a sunny day, you're in the kitchen and the back door is open. A fly flies through the door and into your kitchen. The window doesn't open and as the fly buzzes around, it sees through the window - blue-sky, trees and grass. That's what I'm looking for it thinks, and heads straight for it.

Now you may be surprised to know that flies have no perception of glass! SMACK! It must be quite a shock; however the fly seems to recover quite well and continues buzzing around until it sees through the window - blue-sky, trees, grass and SMACK! They don't learn too well these flies. In fact it will carry on doing this for hours if you let it.

During this time, if you don't want to swat it you will try to wave it towards the open door, but each time you get it close, it will turn and head straight back towards the window.

The fly keeps repeating the behaviour that is getting it nowhere, whilst if it would just go in a different direction the result it needs is just behind it.

So that's the fly test - repeating a behaviour that is getting us nowhere, over and over and over again.

We all need to take a fly test sometimes in our life. "If you want change, change something."

How many people do you know that want changes in their life, but are not prepared to change anything?

➡ People who want to stop smoking, but continue to put cigarettes in their mouth.

➡ People who want to lose weight, but continue to eat too much.

➡ People who want to get fit but don't go to the gym.

➡ People who want to save money, but continue to spend more than they earn.

If you want change, change something. ⬅

People achieving success understand that they have to take responsibility. There are people standing beside the road of life with their thumb out waiting to be taken to where they want to go, whilst others are already driving there.

make it happen

ARE YOU A GOOD HAIRDRESSER OR A FANTASTIC HAIRDRESSER?

The first step on your journey is to decide whether you want to be just a good hairdresser - or a fantastic hairdresser.

How do you want others to think about you? How do you want to be remembered, and most importantly of all what do you want to see when you look in the mirror?

WHERE YOU PUT YOUR FOCUS IS WHERE YOU GET YOUR RESULTS

There is a golden rule in life - where you put your focus is where you get your results.

So if you are focused on being a good hairdresser that's what you will be. But if you focus on being a Fantastic Hairdresser, there is a good chance that you will achieve it.

Part of the reason why this is so important, is that you can look at what you have to change, learn, develop, in order to achieve that goal.

For example, if you decided to go to New York, you would then be able to plan your journey. How you would get there, how long it would take, how much it would cost, what you would have to do to save the money for the fare.

This is also why it is so important that you are specific with your focus. If I just said that I wanted to travel, this is like saying I want to be successful. It is too vague, you can't plan. More importantly you don't activate the filter in your brain that seeks out what you need to do, to achieve your goal.

I even know somebody who decided to test this theory by focusing on finding £1 coins - and he does, constantly. I don't believe I have ever been out with him without him finding at least one, sometimes 2 or 3.

He has been doing this for about 6 years and puts them all in a big jar. One night we counted them - he had over £800!!

What about the Williams sisters - Venus and Serena. If I am honest, I'm not entirely comfortable with the story, but scientifically it is fascinating. Their Dad decided to create tennis champions out of them before they were even born!

His focus was so specific, so positive, (don't just want, or try, to be a fantastic hairdresser - do it - make it happen!) that he created not just one, but two of the top players in the world.

Decide to be a Fantastic Hairdresser - NOW - and you are on the way

Make a commitment now - write in the box below your commitment to being a Fantastic Hairdresser. Use words like, "I will", not "I want", and certainly not "I will try". If you are going to do it, you have to be positive about it. Finally, sign it! Make a real commitment to yourself!!

I hereby commit to the above statement. Signed: _____

characteristics of a fantastic hairdresser

Assuming you have decided to be a fantastic hairdresser, it's time to move on from the foundations which we have dealt with in the first part of the book. Start to look at the characteristics of a Fantastic Hairdresser, and the action you can take to achieve that goal.

I have worked in this industry for 25 years now, and have been privileged to meet and work with some really fantastic hairdressers. All of whom I have been able to learn from.

It was really difficult to pick the characteristics that I felt were the keys. I have narrowed it down to seven, but feel free to add your own if you think I have missed any.

THE FANTASTIC HAIRDRESSER HAS PASSION

It has to start here, because if you don't have a passion for what you do, you can never be fantastic at it. You will learn later that passion for what you do all boils down to how you perceive your job.

THE FANTASTIC HAIRDRESSER GIVES DELIGHT

A fantastic hairdresser will be judged on many things, but surely the most important measurement is if your clients are delighted with you, and what you do for them. That's why I call it customer delight, not customer service.

THE FANTASTIC HAIRDRESSER INSPIRES PEOPLE

If you have passion, knowledge and confidence, then now it is time to look at the most important skill of all - communication. This is not just as a hairdresser, but in life. This skill is so critical to us as human beings, yet I still find it amazing how few people take the time to consciously develop this.

THE FANTASTIC HAIRDRESSER IS AN AMBASSADOR

The fantastic hairdresser is an ambassador for themselves, their salon and the industry. Acting in a professional manner in terms of appearance and behaviour will truly set you apart. You must also recognise that even as a fantastic hairdresser, you need other people. You can't do it on your own, and it's so much more fun as part of a successful team.

THE FANTASTIC HAIRDRESSER IS A PERFORMER

I put this next as I often feel that there are people out there with a passion for their job as well as having the right skills and knowledge, but who are not achieving what they should be because of a lack of confidence in themselves. This is one of the biggest barriers we face in taking the action we need to.

THE FANTASTIC HAIRDRESSER IS ALIVE INSIDE

We all need motivation, and there is nothing better than a pat on the back or a 'thank you' when it is needed.

However you cannot pass over the responsibility for motivation completely, to other people. We have to learn to motivate ourselves if we really want to succeed. Every fantastic hairdresser I have ever met is a positive person.

They have their up's and down's like everybody does, but they understand that they have to move past the bad moments and look forward to the future positively, rather than get caught up in all the staffroom moaning.

THE FANTASTIC HAIRDRESSER IS STILL LEARNING

Obviously passion isn't enough on its own, and has to be backed up by the skills and knowledge to do the job. Clearly these have to be at a high standard, but most importantly as we have already discussed, it is an ongoing commitment to developing that knowledge and those skills.

To do this we have to be creative. Not only is creativity a pre-requisite for this job, but as we have already discussed in the Total Life Concept, it is essential for surviving life today let alone achieving high levels of success. Creativity is simply about having the courage to be wrong, to give your ideas oxygen, let them breathe. Get that idea out of your head and give it a go.

What's the worst that can happen - it doesn't work!

"If you want change
— change something"

Successful people know that
"if it's to be — it's up to me"

choose 3 goals from this chapter that you can take immediate action on:

the fantastic hairdresser has
passion

Why did you become a hairdresser?

I guess there is a chance that you just fell into this industry, that it was not always your passion. Actually, it was that way for me. But training to be a hairdresser is tough. It's hard work, you don't always get the respect you deserve and it's certainly not great money in the early stages. So something must have grabbed you, like it did me. Otherwise why on earth did you carry on!

Was it the creativity, the people, the energy, the excitement, the freedom, the potential you could see or was it one of the many other reasons we do this great job?

Whatever it was, it was enough for you to stick it out, to keep at it. If you don't think you have the passion now, you must have had it at some time, even if it only lasted a few weeks!

Think back to when you had that energy. Do you remember the excitement you felt when you were offered the job you have now?

What happens to that excitement, energy and passion?

We lose our focus. We actually forget what our job is. It becomes all the mundane stuff - which of course every job has - and we lose sight of the elements that excite us.

FOCUS ◄———

We discussed the importance of focus earlier, but this is a different sort of focus.

When we forget why we do what we do, what we love about our job, it is so easy to lose the passion. All of sudden the only things we see are the negative things, the things that irritate us, the stuff we don't like about our job.

Look at it another way. You have probably experienced this with relationships in your life. Whether it is with a romance, family or friends, we have all experienced a time when for some reason all we could see about that person is the stuff that annoyed us. Often, it's small silly insignificant stuff, but it is all we are focused on. It affects everything you feel about that person - negatively. What would happen if you were to re-focus? Think about all the things you love about that person, their strengths rather than their weaknesses.

The lovely things they do, their feelings for you. I guarantee that you will begin to feel differently about that person. Well it's the same with your job. If you have fallen into the trap of only seeing what is wrong with your job, the negative elements - and trust me, there is no such job that does not have those elements - then that is all you will see.

It is a short step from this to hating your job. Becoming miserable and depressed by it, not wanting to go to work. Of course that sort of attitude will affect the way you operate at work so you will not be as successful. Maybe not earn as much money, not have the respect from your colleagues or bosses, then wow, are you on a downward spiral.

Do you know what will happen - you will leave, or get fired, get a new job with all the excitement that you had at the beginning in your previous job. But eventually you will start to feel the same, and the cycle will start all over again.

Do you know that some people spend their whole working life like this, and do you know who they blame - everybody and everything else! We are back to the success pyramid here, "if it's to be - it's up to me" you have to take responsibility, and make the changes that will make a difference - **YOURSELF.**

So let's go back to the beginning - why do you do what you do? Re-focus on that, what you love about your job and you will find it so much easier to deal with the stuff that frustrates you. Spend a few moments now and think about why you wanted to be a hairdresser. Instead of thinking about the things you used hate about hairdressing, start to look at the things you love about it - and you will notice an immediate change in your attitude.

If you find this difficult - if you have really reached a low - persevere - there must be something! Start with little things, and you will get on a roll.

Why I became a hairdresser:

If the last chapter has started to help you develop, or rediscover the passion in your job, then this chapter will help you to keep it.

WHAT IS MY JOB

The first step is to be clear about the difference between what you do and what your job is.

If we met at a party and you asked me what I do - I wouldn't, but I could answer; "I drive up and down motorways, stand in rooms that are too cold or too hot, too large or too small, I make lots of telephone calls, spend time working on a computer."

Now you wouldn't let me get that far. You would interrupt me and say "No, I meant what's your job?".

But you asked me what I do. If you asked me what my job is, I would be able to tell you clearly and concisely, "My job is to communicate with people in such a way as to motivate them to fly!".

To do my job I have to drive up and down motorways, stand in rooms that are too cold etc., but that is not my job. However it is when I am focused on what I do, rather than what my job is, that I lose the passion for what I am doing.

You see I love my job, but sometimes I hate what I do - when I have to stay away from my family, deal with traffic jams, freeze in over-air conditioned seminar rooms.

As I have already said - every job has it's negatives, and if that is where your focus is - then you will be negative.

Shift your focus to what your job is, and it's easy to be passionate about it.

As a hairdresser, you look after customers, shampoo, cut hair, blow dry, deal with problem clients, sweep the floor, unblock sinks, answer the phone, etc.

But your job is simple - YOU MAKE PEOPLE LOOK AND FEEL FANTASTIC EVERY DAY

What a great job! - If only we understood that this is what we are doing every day, we would have so much more fun.

A WORTHWHILE JOB

Your job has to feel worthwhile, for you to keep the passion for it. You can do this with any job; from a dish washer to a road sweeper. There can be job satisfaction in whatever you do - if you choose there to be.

Look beyond what you do, and think about the impact you have on other people's lives.

Think of all the clients you have impacted on, or will in the future.

There must be people out there who clinch great jobs, because their image swung a tight decision. Maybe the start of a beautiful romance came from your client's great new look. Think about what happens when that client walks out of the door - their life carries on in all sorts of ways, but what you do with their hair can affect them so positively.

Spend some time thinking about what your job is, the value of what you are doing, the impact that you have on people and their lives - and remind yourself of what a worthwhile job it is that you do.

Perhaps you have real stories yourself. If not make some up. It doesn't matter how extreme you get because all you are doing, is re-enforcing how great you make people feel on a daily basis.

Now think of a word, phrase or scenario, which really means something to you, as a reminder of how worthwhile your job is. If you can't think of anything, use mine:

As soon as I say to myself "I make people look and feel fantastic", I visualise my clients walking along the road, with a smile on their face, a spring in their step, glancing in shop windows at their reflection, and noticing the admiring looks they get from passers by.

Then next time you forget how worthwhile your job is, when you are feeling a bit down and fed up, remind yourself by thinking of the phrase you have chosen. If you have added a mind movie such as the one I just described, then you find you will automatically start to watch it in your head - and then notice what happens. Notice how much better you feel - immediately.

Another little tip is to write the phrase or word somewhere where you will be frequently looking at it. This will constantly remind your sub-conscious of what your job is, and how much you love it.

the fantastic hairdresser knows how lucky they are

This is something really close to my heart.

Hairdressing is a great job...
...a fantastic job.

We have all had to deal in the past with the judgements that some people make about hairdressers - people who don't understand this great industry: "They only took up hairdressing because they didn't pass their exams at school." "All they ever talk about when they are cutting your hair is what are you doing for your holidays this year?" And so on.

Unfortunately we can be our own worst enemy and can sometimes re-enforce these perceptions. (We will talk about this later in the chapter titled 'The Fantastic Hairdresser is an Ambassador')

However, most of us know that we have to work hard, both physically and mentally, to qualify as a hairdresser. To do this job well, we have to develop many skills, as well as be able to deal with the sheer physicality of spending every day the way we do.

I have certainly found that the communication, understanding and social skills, customer service, and problem solving skills I gained from hairdressing, have helped me enormously in my career and life.

This is a Great Job - and there aren't many others out there that match it

I work with many different industries and professions. Even the "glamorous and exciting" ones that we all at some time wish we were in. But I have very rarely come across another job that matches this one.

Let me explain. First of all, let's look at the type of people you work with. On the whole, and of course there are exceptions to any rule, most of the people that you come across in this industry are; fun, individual, creative, social, exciting, energetic, great people to be around. There are not many jobs that can boast a list like this.

Now let's look at your clients - again, there will always be the 'pain in the bum' sort, but think about it and you know they are the minority.

Most of your customers are nice people, interesting, chatty, friendly and appreciative of what you do for them. You have time to get to know them pretty well, and to really impact on them as well as sometimes get something back in return.

If you have a legal problem, you're sure to come across a solicitor in your chair. You want to buy a house - then talk to that estate agent client of yours. That restaurant you really like, is run by one of your customers - VIP treatment each time you visit.

There are also many instances of the romantic kind that start in the hairdressers chair - sometimes literally!

Now let's look at what you do with those clients - you have the opportunity to be creative - to a certain degree. Of course there will always be core standards, but essentially you have the freedom to do what you like. You and the client make the decision between you, but to a large degree the type of work you do is up to you.

Hairdressing has always been a great job, but it was the business side that used to let it down. We had to put up with bosses who used 'old school' ideas. There was the lack of training and very low wages.

Unfortunately I guess that some of you may be reading this and thinking, "Yes, that's what it's like in my job".

But in general these areas have improved dramatically, with much better management practices and opportunities, really good training, and the opportunity to earn good money now.

My final message to you here is this.

If you are one of the industry's 'whingers', then it is time to stop and realise what a great job this is.

You must take advantage of the opportunities that are there. If you are prepared to work hard, take responsibility, and put the effort in, then you will earn the money that is available, you will benefit from the training. But most of all, you will have fun, enjoy the creativity and potential that this great job can give you.

However if you don't take that responsibility on board, then you will spend the rest of your working life sitting in a staff room somewhere, moaning about everything; asking for pay rises that you don't deserve, depressing your team mates and customers, and forever looking for the greener grass that is right there underneath your feet. It's a great job - if you want it to be!

"Make your clients look and feel — fantastic"

Recognise the difference between your job - and what you do

choose 3 goals from this chapter that you can take immediate action on:

4

the fantastic hairdresser

gives delight

I am sure that in your salon - the term customer service is well known. You know that customer service is one of the most important principles of a successful salon and a successful hairdresser.

I am sure that you provide good service to your customers. I know that you know what good service is, from greeting the clients properly, through to a good consultation and making sure they are happy and comfortable throughout their visit. You probably have lots of little extras for the client as well - a refreshment menu perhaps, sweets and flowers at reception, daily newspapers as well as magazines.

However, it's not enough - good service is no longer enough

It's no longer enough because it's not special anymore - it's expected! We have to give more than service now; it's time to move up to Customer Delight. But what is the difference?

FROM CUSTOMER SERVICE TO CUSTOMER DELIGHT

It's simple; customer service is about the important procedures and standards that you have in your salon. The way you greet clients, answer the phone, use their name, take their coat, smile, escort them through the salon etc. These procedures and standards are critical, as they help to ensure consistency, but they are not the whole story.

Customer Delight is the way that you do those things. It is your attitude that really makes the difference.

It's not enough just to perform the standards. That's like an actor just saying their lines, or an artist just singing a song. There are plenty of people who can sing a song, but performing it - performing in it such a way as to grab the hearts of millions of people - as some artists do, that is much more than singing a song.

The Fantastic Hairdresser does much more than carry out the standards.

You have to live it, believe it, feel it and I suppose most of all you have to want to do it. You have to enjoy making people feel good.

▶ HOW DO YOU KNOW YOU ARE ACHIEVING IT?

When a performer gets a standing ovation, it lets them know they have made the audience feel good.

Well there are two ways a hairdresser gets feedback that they are giving delight to their customers. The first is that the client comes back for more, and the second is how high your average bill is! Why average bill? Because this is a measurement of what your client's hair looks like when they walk out of the salon - the more colour, movement, treatments you are giving, the more clients you have leaving the salon looking fantastic.

It is also a measurement of how they look a few weeks later - how they manage their hair themselves. If they have the right products, they can keep their hair looking good without you. Without the products, they would really struggle. Could you create the look for them if you didn't have the right products to use? Then how on earth can you expect your clients to?

Look at your average bill. This is your weekly take divided by how many clients you have done. If it's not at least £5 above your cut and finish price, then you are just not giving your clients that extra delight that they want. You do not have enough clients walking out of your salon with a little bit of colour, having had a lovely scalp massage and hair treatment, or with the right products to maintain their style. This is the minimum though:

If you really want to be a fantastic hairdresser, then set your sights higher. You will be amazed how high your average bill can go if you really focus on making your clients look and feel great, put in the effort and work you need to.

CUSTOMER SERVICE IS ABOUT STANDARDS

CUSTOMER DELIGHT IS ABOUT PASSION

IT'S ABOUT MAKING PEOPLE FEEL GOOD

the fantastic hairdresser knows - it's not the lions that bite

To give Customer Delight, you have to be able to give people what they want. Do they want to chat about what you are up to, or what is happening in their life? Or do they just want to be left alone? Do they enjoy flattery or are they embarrassed by it? Are they in a hurry or do they want to be pampered?

You have to know what is going on inside their heads, if you are going to give them what they want.

PAY ATTENTION TO TINY THINGS

Be aware of the smallest things. Know that the tiniest detail is critical. To achieve Customer Delight, you have to be aware of what the client is thinking and feeling - you have to tune in to what they are aware of.

Just take a moment one day and look at your salon, look at the service you give personally, through the client's eyes. What things would you not tolerate if you were a customer?

The interesting thing here is that most of the things that go wrong are the small things - I call them gnat bites.

Have you ever been bitten by a lion? Probably not. Have you ever been bitten by a gnat, or a midge, or a mosquito? I bet you have. Don't worry about the lion - it's the little things that will get you!

Well that's the same in service. I doubt if you have lost too many clients from a lion bite - a major customer service disaster. But I know you have all lost customers through gnat bites.

It works like this. You are on holiday, sunbathing by the pool and you are bitten by a mosquito. It is mildly irritating, annoying, but certainly not enough for you to leave your sun bed and move elsewhere. Two bites - a bit more annoying, but still not enough. Three bites - I'm not happy now - four bites I'm getting angry, 5,6,7,8 I've had enough I'm going.

That's exactly what happens to the little, seemingly insignificant things that occur every day in your salon. They gradually start to wind your client up, to the point where you may never see them again.

Increase your awareness, and stop the gnat bites.

WALK THE SALON

There is a great way to do this:-

- At the end of the day, before you go home one evening 'walk your salon'.

- Get yourself a note pad and then starting from outside the door of the salon, step inside.

- As you do this, think about how you would like to be greeted if you were a client, and how long you would be prepared to stand waiting to be seen. What annoys you in this situation when you are a customer, say in a restaurant or shop?

- Now ask yourself what you can do to improve this moment - this potential gnat bite.
  Write it down in your note pad.

- Carry on throughout the salon, following the route you would take if you were a client, spotting all the potential gnat bites you can find, and asking yourself the same question.

- Go from reception to the waiting area and from there to the consultation. Then walk to the backwash, before heading back to the chair for whatever service the client might be having.

- Finally think about how the client leaves the salon.

This exercise really begins to raise your awareness of the little stuff, which will make a difference as to how you deal with your clients. Do it every couple of months to keep that level high. If you have filled in the note pad on the way round, you will have a catalogue of potential disaster areas in your salon, which you can start to improve on.

If you want to be a Fantastic Hairdresser, do something about the things that are letting you and your salon down - take responsibility - don't just sit there moaning - do something!

the fantastic hairdresser does it right - consistently

Perhaps one of the most important things about Customer Delight is trust. When you are operating at such a high level, your clients will have so much trust in you that they will give you the most valuable gift they can - a new client!

Recommendation, word of mouth, is the single most important way to build your column and achieve the success you desire.

How do you get high recommendation levels? - From trust. You may have a client that loves you doing their hair and has been coming to you for years, but they don't recommend other people to you. Believe it or not, this is because they don't trust you.

HOW DO YOU GAIN TRUST FROM PEOPLE?

TRUST IS ABOUT CONSISTENCY

Let me tell you about a local restaurant of mine. It's in a lovely position, overlooking the Thames in West London. It is literally five minutes stroll from my house. It has a balcony overlooking the river, and there is no better place to have breakfast and watch all the Sunday morning activity.

Sound good? Well let me tell you a bit more.

The service is not bad, but it's by no stretch of the imagination good either. The food is ok, although we often have to send it back because it's not warm enough. It seems there are two chefs; and the quality of the food depends on which one is working.

Sometimes they don't open the balcony, even if it's a lovely sunny day. (When I ask why it is closed, the impression I get is that they just can't be bothered).

So why do I go back you must be asking? Because I like sitting on the balcony watching the world go by on a Sunday morning. I choose to tolerate their inconsistencies, because I like going there and it's close by.

I wonder how many of your clients put up with being kept waiting, moody staff, music too loud, etc, because they like the way you do their hair, or because you are conveniently just around the corner.

However - here is the critical point. Even though I choose to tolerate it, even though I still go there on a Sunday morning - if you asked me to recommend a restaurant in my area, I wouldn't dream of sending you there - because I can't trust them to get it right when you visit.

I DON'T TRUST THEM. I know they can do it right, but they don't do it right consistently.

Trust comes from consistency, and being dependable and it's only when you are trusted that clients will recommend new clients. Your team and your clients trust you when they know they can rely on you.

You have probably agreed with much of what I have said so far in this book, you may even feel that you do everything I have said so far.

You may do - in fact; I guess that many of you do.

However my question is not whether you do what you have to, to give your clients customer delight - it's whether you do it consistently, time after time, and day after day.

If you are inconsistent, people cannot rely on you, you will let your team mates down, and your clients will be fed up. They may they decide to tolerate your inconsistent time keeping, mood swings, attitude etc., because they like you cutting their hair - but they will not recommend other clients to you.

In a later chapter, we will look at personal standards.

Standards are the key to consistency. Your salon's standards - even if you don't like them - are essential for the consistency of what you are providing, and your personal standards help you to stay up there - at the top - as a fantastic hairdresser.

"Bring back the "WOW" factor"

Service is about standards — delight is about passion

choose 3 goals from this chapter that you can take immediate action on:

5

the fantastic hairdresser

inspires people

the fantastic hairdresser asks questions

Communication is probably the most important skill there is.

Not just as a Fantastic Hairdresser, but in every part of your life. However, it is amazing how many people do nothing to develop this skill. It's as though we learnt how to communicate through growing up at home and school - and that's it.

There is so much to learn about this skill - yes it's a skill - yet we do very little to develop it. Perhaps the golden rule of communication and one that is often overlooked by poor communicators, is that it always involves two or more parties.

A poor communicator is so wrapped up in what they want to say, what they believe is right, that they forget the other party has opinions and views as well.

It is essential to gain an understanding of your clients - to get to know what makes them tick, what they are really looking for from a visit to your salon. You have to listen to people, because when you do, you will find out exactly what they are asking from you. Then it's easy to make them happy, by providing what they want.

I have always maintained that the most important tool a hairdresser has, is the consultation. It really makes the difference between the good hairdresser and the fantastic hairdresser.

A good consultation should be a compromise between what you know, and what your client wants. To do that - you need information. You have to have something to work from.

IF YOU DON'T ASK, YOU DON'T GET!

If you want information - ask questions. There are three types of questions you must use more. Firstly, the one's you have probably heard about many times, although you may not be using them.

Conversational questions. They are simply questions that it is impossible to answer yes or no to. Your client will have to give an answer back that starts a conversation.

The questions always start with these words:

▶ **WHAT, WHY, WHEN, WHO, HOW, WHERE and WHICH**

Try it. It's impossible to answer yes or no. They have to give information back, which is what you need from your client, to be able to give them what they want.

The next questions you have to practice are called 'probing questions'. This is when you ask your question again if you do not get the information you need. But rephrase it; ask it in a different manner. Don't just ask the question repeatedly, getting frustrated by the lack of information you get.

The most important quote I know about communication is:

"The archer doesn't blame the target when they miss"

If the message is not getting through, or if you are not getting the information you want - your aim is wrong. Don't blame the target, change your aim. If the questions you are asking are not giving you what you want, then ask again, and again, different questions, until you get the information you need.

Part of this process is to 'question the vague'. Sometimes people are not specific enough with their answers, so question what is vague. Look at the answer below - I have put the unspecific parts that need questioning, in bold.

"How is your hair at the moment?"
"Oh **not bad**, I do have some **problems** with it **occasionally**, sometimes it **feels strange**, and I can't **manage** it. Mind you I **don't always look after** it as well as I **should**."

Probe those parts of the answer, and you will get the information you need to really help this client.

Finally, try asking questions that you know the answer to. You may look at a client's hair and think that it's in bad condition and that they are probably swimming regularly in a chlorine pool. Any self respecting hairdresser can spot this a mile off, but instead of telling them that their hair is in bad condition, ask them how they feel about the condition of their hair. They will probably say that it is not very good at the moment, as they are doing a lot of swimming. You can now respond to their answer - the problem they are giving you - rather than telling them what is wrong.

The simple advice is - if you want to know something - ask!

Now that you are getting information from your client, you have to listen to what they tell you - really listen!

Communication is one of the most important skills in life and listening is the most important communication skill. Therefore, I guess that makes listening pretty important!

There are two types of listening you must practice. Firstly using your ears. Think about the following rules of good listening and ask yourself how you do.

1. Give complete attention and focus to the person speaking
2. Give good eye contact, and use appropriate body language
3. Make listening noises to encourage, "Mm, aha, really"
4. Think only about what they are saying, not about what you are going to say when they have finished
5. Never interrupt
6. Never finish peoples sentences
7. Think briefly about what they have said and your opinions on it, before responding.

How did you do? Is it time to start learning to listen?

THE LISTENING SWITCH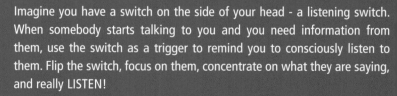

Imagine you have a switch on the side of your head - a listening switch. When somebody starts talking to you and you need information from them, use the switch as a trigger to remind you to consciously listen to them. Flip the switch, focus on them, concentrate on what they are saying, and really LISTEN!

If you get into the habit of doing this, it will start to happen naturally. But start now. You have people talking to you every day - it's a great opportunity for you to develop one of the most important skills in life.

▶ LISTENING WITH YOUR EYES

This is fascinating. When you learn to use your eyes to listen to people, it is amazing how much information you can get. There are two areas I want you to think about here.

Firstly, you have to understand which part of their brain someone is using to process information, which then allows you to communicate much more effectively with them.

There are three ways we all process information inside our heads.

We visualise it, hear it, or we feel it. If someone is using the visual part of their brain to listen to you, they will not understand you - they will not SEE what you mean - if you do not use visual references when explaining something.

You need to know how they are thinking. Watch peoples' eyes and they give you all the clues you need. When someone is visualising they either gaze off into the distance, or more usually, they glance upwards.

If someone is listening inside his or her head, they will glance to the side, and when they are experiencing a feeling, they will look down. If you bother to take notice of this, and adjust your communication accordingly, you will be amazed by the results.

If you are trying to discuss colour with a client by telling them how they will look, or what people will say, but they are constantly glancing downwards, then you need to talk to them about emotions. Discuss how they will feel and you will start to get their attention.

As you practice this with your clients, you will become skilled at knowing how people are thinking. From this you'll be able to match your communication and obtain the best results. This is rapport, and it is critical to good communication.

Secondly, become more aware of your own, and other peoples' body language. It's not a perfect science, but it does give you many pointers that are very helpful to great communication.

Learn to recognise when someone is nervous, or unhappy. Start to recognise if your client is in a hurry, before the complaints start. I would strongly recommend Alan Pease's great book 'Body Language'. It's a lot of fun and will give you some real insights into what people are telling you.

uses positive communication

The language we use has a powerful impact on both the people we are communicating with and ourselves. We do listen to ourselves!

The effect that language has on the way we operate is amazing. When you understand it, you become very careful about what you say to yourself and to others.

The unconscious part of the brain that processes the information you receive, from yourself or others, does not have the capability to make decisions. It simply looks in its memory banks for the definition it has for those words and acts accordingly.

Put your right arm up in the air now. OK, put it down now.

Now, assuming you just did that - this is what happened. Information gets to your brain via one or more of your senses. In this case, you read it, so it was through sight, but if I had said it, then it would have been through your ears.

That information was then processed and you acted upon it. Some of that took place at a conscious level - maybe you had to take a moment to think about right or left - but most of it happened at an un-conscious or sub conscious level. Your brain worked the muscles needed to complete that task, but you were not aware of it - it was not at a conscious level.

This is obviously happening all the time. What it tells us, is that there is some sort of 'brain dictionary' that understands "right arm up" and what it means.

Do you understand Japanese, or Russian? What if I asked you to do the same thing in a language you didn't understand? What would happen - nothing! Because your brain would not understand the words and so would not be able to process them.

Your brain understands the words that are fed into it and reacts accordingly.

This is so important as it explains why listening to positive communication starts to make you feel more positive but....... the same is true for negative communication - you feel more negative. If you say to yourself "I'm feeling really knackered", your brain understands what "knackered" means - it knows what it feels like - and so will then act in that way, making you feel even more knackered.

Start to listen to people and you will notice how negative we can be in what we say to ourselves, and to other people. Unfortunately, you will see this a lot with children. If you tell a child they are "bad" for long enough, what will you get? A bad child!

There are three things I want you to change, to improve the words you use.

Firstly, start to make your language more helpful. Use positive alternatives such as "I need to stay awake", rather than "I mustn't fall asleep". "Make sure I remember..." not "Make sure I don't forget".

It's interesting to notice what happens when you use words like "don't", or "mustn't". Say to yourself: "Don't think of an elephant". What happens? You think of an elephant! In fact you can't "not think of an elephant", without thinking of one!

So when you say, "don't forget" your brain thinks about forgetting, and what is the brain dictionary's definition of forget?

Notice how some people respond to a simple "How are you?" "Not bad" is a favourite answer - all your brain understands is "bad"! How many times a day does that that happen - everyday? What a great message you are giving yourself, let alone the people who are asking.

Write a list of the negative words or phrases that you use and find positive alternatives for them. You will notice a dramatic difference in the effect your communication has on both yourself and others.

Secondly, always talk about behaviour that you want to change - about yourself or someone else - in the past tense.

If you say to a client, "I know you don't have colour on your hair, but I want to tell you about ..." all you are doing is reminding her that she doesn't have colour.

However if you said, "I know you haven't had colour on your hair in the past but we have a fantastic new product..." Instead of re-enforcing the negative by using the present tense, you have put it in the past. Your client is now thinking about "the fantastic new product". It's a very subtle tool, but incredibly effective.

Finally, tell stories to your clients using a third party reference.

Using a third party in a story is a gentler way of introducing an idea to your client.

Tell a story about a customer of yours who used to colour her hair at home, but one day decided to have it done in the salon. Talk about how thrilled she was with the result. You will be surprised how easy, and effective, this is.

"The archer doesn't blame the target when they miss"

If your message doesn't get through, it's your aim that's wrong

choose 3 goals from this chapter that you can take immediate action on:

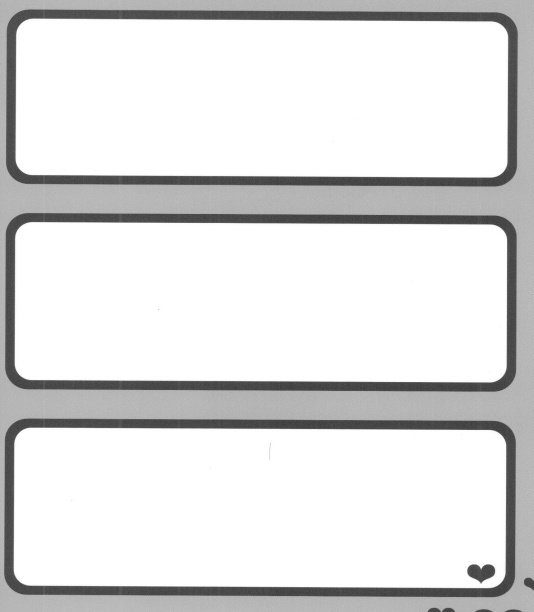

the fantastic hairdresser

is an **Ambassador**

the fantastic hairdresser understands it's a business

THE AMBASSADOR

We sometimes as human beings make judgements. We notice how people dress, talk, act, and treat others. We shouldn't do it, but we do - what would you think of a dentist with bad teeth, a fat fitness instructor, or a doctor who smokes.

A fantastic hairdresser recognises that they are an ambassador. Primarily they are an ambassador for themselves; however, you have to recognise that they are also an ambassador for their salon.

A while ago, I was walking behind a young guy who was drinking from a can. He finished, and threw the can at a bin on the street. It missed. He saw it miss but carried on walking leaving it on the pavement. I then noticed that his t-shirt was branded with a salon name and logo. As he stepped through the door of that salon, I made a judgement! Not just about him, but about the type of salon who would employ someone who drops litter.

Now I know better than to make judgements like that - and you might say that it's not fair, which would be true. But I'm human, and that's how most of us would respond.

As well as your behaviour reflecting on yourself and your salon, you must also be an ambassador for your industry. I have attended many awards ceremonies where fellow hairdressers let us down by being too loud at the wrong times and drowning out what is happening on stage for example. With members of the press attending, people from other industries, parents, friends etc. attending, it doesn't exactly portray the professional image the industry is now known for.

The fantastic hairdresser is an ambassador for themselves, their salon and their industry.

From observing successful team members at work, from asking them questions, it has become crystal clear to me that they all have one thing in common regarding their attitude towards the job that they do, and the company that they work for.

They understand it's a business.

Hairdressing is a creative job, but it is also a business and when you truly understand that, you will understand so much more about how to be successful within this industry. Look at the companies that have achieved the amazing success they have over the last ten years and you will see that they have evolved from hairdressing salon - to hairdressing business.

As creative people, we would all love to be free to do whatever we like. Wear what we want and take as long as we need on a haircut etc. However, if the business does not have standards, then you can't achieve consistency, and without that, you will lose clients.

WORK AS THOUGH YOU WERE THE BOSS

Imagine if the salon you worked in was your own. Would you operate in the same way?

You would want things to be right of course. You would want the clients to receive the highest standards. So then understand why your boss is passionate about everyone doing it right – and why they get so frustrated sometimes when that isn't happening!

As an ambassador of your salon and your industry, understand that hairdressing is a business, a business that has to be profitable. A business that has to keep clients, and that has bills to pay.

It comes as a shock to many people to learn that even in an efficiently run business, 60-65 pence in every pound the salon ever takes goes straight back out in wages, NI, and stock!

That leaves 35 pence from each pound to pay all the bills – rent, rates, insurance, accountants, electricity, laundry, refreshments, marketing, and training. That's before any profit comes out of the business.

So next time you want a pay rise, or a budget for a photo shoot, remember hairdressing is a business. You must make a good case to persuade your boss that it is worth it, and have some understanding

the fantastic hairdresser has high values

As an ambassador, you have to have high personal standards.

We have talked about salon standards and service standards to ensure consistency. But what about you? How do you make sure that you perform at a high level consistently?

YOUR VALUES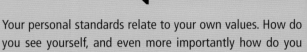

Your personal standards relate to your own values. How do you see yourself, and even more importantly how do you want others to perceive you?

The answers to those questions are the starting point for your personal standards.

Imagine you were listening in on the following conversations and the parties concerned didn't know you were listening.

1. Some clients of yours talking about you
2. Some clients of the salon, but not yours, talking about you
3. Some team members talking about your attitude at work
4. Your boss talking about your attitude at work

First of all, think about what you would love to hear them say about you.

Now think about what they might say that would be horrible to hear! What you know they could say - if you were really honest with yourself!

You know what I mean - you may never admit it to anyone else, but deep down you know that - for example - you can be moody, and can bring that into work, which can upset people in your team. How would you feel if you heard a comment like this about yourself?

"Well they are a nice person, and I really like them, but sometimes they can be so moody I just can't be doing with all the drama!"

I think if you heard someone say that, you would have to look closely at yourself and question whether your behaviour is doing you any favours. Or, perhaps you hear a client telling a friend how good you are, but because you are so slow and constantly keep her waiting she is thinking of moving salons!

Remember, responsibility.
If you want change - change something

Don't look at other people, don't point the finger of blame, and equally don't feel sorry for yourself either. Just decide what you are going to do about it - and do it!

These questions will help you to recognise your values, the level you want to operate at, and the level you certainly don't want to. From there you can start to establish the sort of personal standards that will start to propel you towards your goal of being a fantastic hairdresser. Here you go, answer them now.

YOU OVERHEAR:

1. Some clients of yours talking about you

Love to hear them say:

Hate to hear them say:

2. Some clients of the salon, but not yours, talking about you

Love to hear them say:

Hate to hear them say:

3. Some team members talking about your attitude at work

Love to hear them say:

Hate to hear them say:

4. Your boss talking about your attitude at work

Love to hear them say:

Hate to hear them say:

Even a fantastic hairdresser can't do it on their own.

The more support you have from other people, the easier life is. Many of us try to take on the world alone - but it's so much easier if you have the support of others.

To achieve the high standards of a Fantastic Hairdresser you have to begin to understand that everyone in the team - however old or inexperienced they are - plays a part in making sure that the client leaves your salon "looking and feeling fantastic".

The key to this support is your communication with your colleagues. Have you ever wondered why some stylists can always get someone to shampoo for them, whilst others moan that they never get any help?

Positive Feedback

Everyone loves positive feedback. Some people pretend that they don't - but they do. They just have a belief somewhere that says it's cool to be negative, to not show any emotion, to think that anything positive is shallow and can't be trusted. However, underneath all that, they will still respond to positive communication.

I'm not talking about "motivational guru speak" here. Just simply the difference you get with people when you communicate positively rather than negatively.

Imagine a situation where someone in your team is working hard, but not hard enough to achieve the goal. Maybe their results are leaving them low down in the league table, and so affecting the team goal.

Let them know: "I recognise that you are working hard - but we are not achieving our goal". They will agree that they need to do more.

But tell them they are not working hard enough and they will become negative and defensive.

The way you communicate with your colleagues, your team, is essential for achieving your goals. Although we shouldn't let it happen, it is inevitable that the moods and emotions of the people we work with will affect us.

The happier everyone is - the more positive the team is - and you will all have more fun. The more fun you have, the easier it is to be successful.

Therefore, if your communication is causing problems, upsetting people or making them negative - it is ultimately bouncing back to you.

Great communication is all about understanding. The more you understand people, the easier it is to know what makes them tick.

Get to your know your team mates. Not just the ones you are friends with - in fact, make a real effort with the people you don't know as well, or even think that you don't like!

What are their interests, their views, what are their goals and their dreams?

To do this well though, you have to be in the right state of mind. Look at some of the judgements and assumptions we make sometimes. They don't allow us to communicate well.

Recognise that other people have strengths, have a right to their opinions - even if you disagree with them. They also have weaknesses - but doesn't everybody? In fact don't you?

It doesn't matter how old someone is - can you learn from a 6, 8,12 year old? Of course you can. So why do we think we can't learn from a 17 year old? Do you make judgements on peoples past mistakes - how would you feel if other people judged you solely on the mistakes you have made?

Finally do you listen to people - or is it not really worth it, because you are always right anyway!!

When you are making these sorts of judgements or assumptions, you can't listen to what people say. Be confident in yourself, your knowledge and your views, but recognise that others have something to offer as well - as well as the basic human right to be treated with respect. Yes - even teenagers!!

As your state of mind changes, you will find that your communication with people improves. You gain more understanding, praising them and recognising the effort they put into the team's goals.

All of which takes you closer to the "holy grail" of success in what you do:

The clear understanding that you are part of a team - a team of people working together to achieve a shared goal - that you need the support of others - that it's ok that you can't do everything, but that you will always have something to offer the team - that everyone, yes everyone, has a role to play in making the team successful, and the job we do, enjoyable and fun!

"Work as if it was your own business"

Be proud of your job, your company and your industry

choose 3 goals from this chapter that you can take immediate action on:

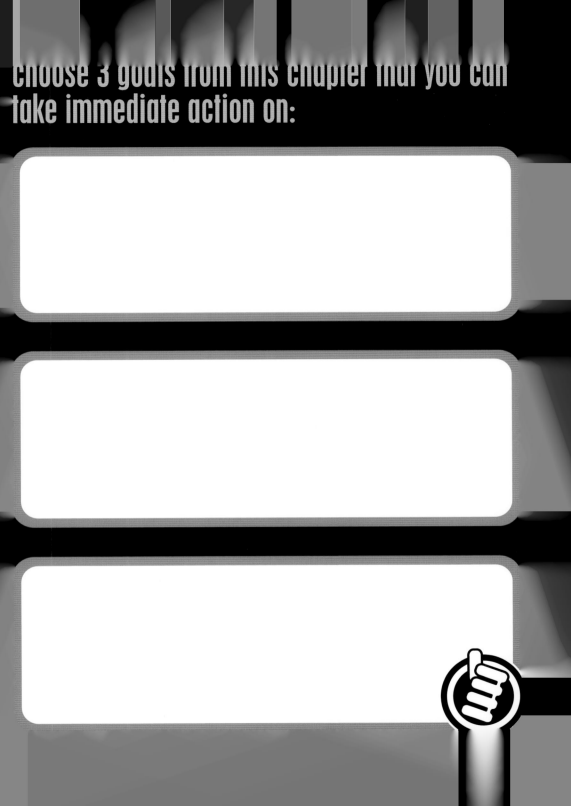

the fantastic hairdresser

7

is a performer

the fantastic hairdresser uses dogashi!

DOGASHI? What is that? DOGASHI is a wonderful ancient eastern technique that has the most amazing impact on your ability to take action in your life.

Taking action is not always as easy as it seems. We all intend to do the things that we decide to, but so often it doesn't happen. Not just the big things in life either. Think about the times you were going to send someone a thank you card - but didn't, or what about those phone calls that you need to make, but keep putting off?

THE VOICES! ⬅

I remember a visit to my dentist once, many years ago, before I knew about DOGASHI. I was late for my appointment, and I knew that I had messed up her day. She was really nice about it, but I still felt guilty, and as I lay there in the chair, I remembered that there was a flower stall outside the front door. As an apology for being late and a thank you for being so nice about it, I decided to get her some flowers. A nice thing to do I'm sure you agree.

Then the voices started!

You know - the voices in our heads that start to talk us out of things, which introduce doubts and fear. "She'll think you fancy her if you get her flowers", "She'll be embarrassed", "You'll be embarrassed next time you see her", "What will the receptionist think". Recognise any of those? Well that's what started in my head when I decided to get her some flowers.

The sad thing is, I let them win - I didn't get the flowers!

If you want to take action - even with the little things in life - then you have to deal with those voices, and shut them up. You see, most of the time the voices are wrong!! I don't think she would have thought I fancied her, or been embarrassed, I think she would have been over the moon! It would have been a nice thing to happen on a stressful busy day.

SO, HOW DOES DOGASHI WORK?

It silences the voices and enables you to step past them and do what you want to do. It helps you to learn something, from this book perhaps, and put it into action - without worrying what other people say about your new behaviour. It could help you to overcome the peer pressure; that is making you drink too much, party too hard, or take drugs that don't help you. You know what I mean. We have all been in a situation where we have wanted to go home early from a night out. Or someone wanted us to do something we didn't want to - but the voices are telling us that our friends will think us boring, etc.

DOGASHI is simply a way to remind yourself that they are only voices in your head. Sure, sometimes they might be right and you should listen to them, but in my experience DOGASHI always helps me recognise the ones that are just knocking me back, the ones that are stopping me taking the action I should do.

OK I FIBBED!!

Sorry - I fibbed a bit about DOGASHI. It isn't really an ancient eastern technique. I just thought that it added a bit of intrigue. It does sound like it though doesn't it - "DOGASHI" - but I actually made it up! I wanted a word that I could use to shut the voices up, and DOGASHI is actually a statement that I was using, shortened down to make it easier, and perhaps nicer to use.

You see DOGASHI is short for - DOn't Give A SHIt! That's what you have to say to those voices sometimes when they are trying to stop you taking action - DOGASHI - I don't give a shit - I'm still going to do it!

THE MOST IMPORTANT THING TO REMEMBER ABOUT DOGASHI

I am sure you understand the manner in which I mean this statement. However unfortunately, it does seem that there are people who do occasionally get the wrong idea. As some of you will remember, DOGASHI first started life as DOGASH. It was later pointed out to me that it read as: DOG, ASH which didn't have a very pleasant ring to it!

There are a few trainers out there using it as their own, and as DOG-ASH I might add! But the really important thing that does seem to have been overlooked by some of them, is that DOGASHI is not about other people.

It's not about being arrogant or aggressive. You are not saying that you don't care about other people, or their feelings. No, DOGASHI is simply about getting rid of the voices in your head that are holding you back. When you use it, you instinctively know that those voices are wrong.

There you go - DOGASHI - try it, it's fantastic, shut those voices up and have the confidence to take action.

the fantastic hairdresser **changes their mind**

MIND MOVIES ⬅

Fear is in our mind, sometimes it's real, sometimes it isn't, and even when it is real - it is still only in our heads.

We have all been home alone, watching a spooky movie and heard a sound somewhere in the house. What happens - your mind takes over. It starts to spiral out of control as you begin to worry about what the noise might mean. Before you know it, you are prowling around the house with a carving knife in your hand kicking open doors as you look for the intruder - that isn't there!

See what we do to ourselves.

Most of the time, the things we fear may happen to us, are nothing more than a figment of our imagination.

Have you ever seen a client at the reception desk and decided for some reason that she is scary? Then you find out that she has booked in to see you tomorrow.

Some people will start to worry about her, watching movies in their mind (I call these mind movies) of her not liking her hair, thinking you are incompetent and complaining about you. The more you watch this movie, the less confident you will be.

There are two results here. You will either find that you were wrong and she is a lovely sweet person - or maybe she really is a bit troublesome.

The interesting thing is though, because you have worried so much about it, your confidence levels will be low, and she will be much more trouble than she would have been if you had come across as confident and assertive.

So learn to change the movies. Next time your mind is running away with you and you are watching a mind movie that is taking away your confidence - change your mind, and watch a different movie.

If you see yourself talking to a client about colour and the movie you watch always ends with them saying no, that will affect your confidence and they probably will say no.

Change the movie - be your own film director. Watch yourself talking confidently to your client about colour, see her being excited by it, and then give it a happy ending! See your client walking out of the salon looking and feeling fantastic, because of the colour you have given her.

This movie will change the way you are feeling, making you more positive and confident about what you are going to do. There are no guarantees - other than if you feel better about yourself, you will perform better, and then stand a better chance of success.

Jot down here some of the mind movies that you find yourself watching at work that you know aren't doing you any good. Then create an alternative movie, a new, better one. A movie that you know would give you more confidence in that situation.

Negative movie:

Positive Alternative:

Negative movie:

Positive Alternative:

Julia Roberts once told a group of drama students that she could get terribly nervous at auditions.

When a student asked how she deals with those nerves, she replied, "I'm an actress - I act. I act confident, and the more you act confident, the more confident you become."

We have all done this in other ways. Maybe you are feeling tired or hung-over at work, but you know that you can't be like that in front of the client, so you pretend you are OK. You act. Isn't it amazing how you can change the way you feel?

Quite quickly you will feel fine. Because you started to act that way, you began to feel like that.

Or maybe you have done it the other way! When you were younger, you didn't want to go to school one day, so you pretended that you didn't feel well. You acted ill. In fact, you may have turned in such an Oscar winning performance that you actually started to feel ill.

An actor isn't sad, they are just acting sad. They don't love that person, they are acting.

However - they do it so well we believe it. They are able to get into the right state of mind to make us believe it.

To do that, firstly they have to make themselves believe it. They get themselves so into the role, that they actually start to believe the part they are playing - which then makes us believe it.

That is what happens when you act. If you act confidently, then you start to feel confident which in turn makes others feel that you are confident.

Your state of mind, your attitude, is determined by the movies you watch in your head. When you realise that all you have to do is change the movie, then it's easy.

Try some of the following exercises today:

Walk down the street as though you are a really important person. Notice how your posture is different. A straight back, positive steps, looking up, not down at the floor. Come on, you know how a VIP would walk along the street, act as though you were like that.

Now start to recognise how it makes you feel. What about other peoples' reactions to you? Are they different?

Go into work today and act as though you feel fantastic. You are so happy; you have just received some great news. I bet you have a great day, and your smiles will rub off onto everyone else.

Finally, try this at home on your own; otherwise you might be locked up! Just start laughing - a fake laugh - you are acting. It helps if you think of something funny that has happened to you or one of your friends.

Now keep going, laughing harder and louder. Keep it going for a few minutes then stop, and take notice of how you feel. It is a scientific fact that laughing releases endorphins into your system, which make you feel great. Interestingly, this also boosts your immune system. Even fake laughing will do this.

Try these and any others you want, to prove to yourself that by acting you can convince your body and mind to feel and operate differently.

However, if you are talking yourself out of doing these exercises, - remember - DOGASHI!! Shut those voices up and just do it!

"You're on stage — act like it!"

Your audience is watching you, all of the time

choose 3 goals from this chapter that you can take immediate action on:

8

the fantastic hairdresser
is alive inside

the fantastic hairdresser **knows where they are going**

One of the most popular parts of Take Control, our life skills seminar, is 'Alive Inside'. I show people that if they change the way they are feeling on the inside - it has a powerful effect on the way they are operating on the outside.

If you want to be alive on the outside, living your life to the full, then you have to be alive on the inside!

Self-motivation - we all need to be motivated, and enjoy praise and encouragement from others, but if you have taken anything at all from this book, surely it is the fact that "if it's to be - it's up to me".

You have to take responsibility for your life, and what happens in it. The same is true for your motivation.

YOUR GOALS

This starts with knowing where you are going. How can you be motivated to achieve something if you don't know what that something is?

How can you work out what you have to do to get somewhere - if you don't know where you are going?

There are two types of goals that make the difference. The first is your salon goal - your team goal. The reason why this comes first, is simply that we all lose our motivation at times, lose focus on what we are trying to achieve, and it is at those times that your team is most vital to you.

Nobody wants to let the team down, and when you realise that your lack of focus on your own personal goals is affecting the team, it's easy to regain the motivation again.

This brings us to the second type of goal - your own personal objectives. These should always be connected to the team goal in some way. Either it is something that you need to improve in order for the team to achieve its goal, or it's a strength of yours that you can offer the team.

THE RULES OF GOALS

There are some simple rules that will give you the best chance of achieving your goals.

The first and most important is the understanding that where you put your focus is where you get your results. A good example of this is when you are buying a car. The moment you decide - focus - on the make and model you want, you will see it everywhere.

It is because of this fact that the second rule of goals is so important - be specific. It's no good saying that you want to be more successful. You have to be precise. For example, I hope that you are thinking about becoming more of a fantastic hairdresser after reading this book. But how will you know when you have achieved it? What is the measurement? The term Fantastic Hairdresser is too vague on its own.

In chapter 4, I suggested that average bill was a good way of measuring how good a hairdresser you are, as it measures how many of your clients are leaving the salon looking and feeling fantastic. Linked with a high repeat business figure, this is one of the best ways of measuring how good you are!

So instead of just saying that you want to be a fantastic hairdresser - decide how high you want your average bill to be. Make it a level that takes you to the very peak of your industry. NOW YOU HAVE A GOAL.

Now you need to put some sort of time line to it. When will you achieve this by? Remember be specific and positive about your goal and you will have a much greater chance of achieving it.

The next two pages put the icing on the cake as far as goals are concerned. Remember - where you put your focus is where you get your results - so if you want average results - then set average goals.

However, if you want spectacular in your life - then you had better start setting spectacular goals!

the fantastic hairdresser has no limits

NO LIMITS!

I have a belief in my life, it is simply that

THE ONLY LIMITS THAT EXIST, ARE THE LIMITS I PUT ON MYSELF

There is a wonderful quote from Henry Ford. "If you think you can, or you think you can't - you're right!"

Be careful of thinking that the money you take in a week is all you can take. If you think you can't increase your average bill - you're right, you can't. But when you think you can, you will start looking for ways to do it.

Maybe you think you aren't very creative - you are - you just have to believe it. Want to buy a property, book your dream holiday, buy that car, but you can't because you don't earn enough?

Believe you can, and then you will find a way. The only limits that exist are the limits you put on yourself.

Remember the 10% rule we discussed earlier in the book - the millionaire hairdresser?

Work it out for yourself, make a start now and build your strong financial future.

The 10% rule

10% of my take home pay:

50% of my tips:

Total saved per week:

Total saved per month (x 4):

Total saved per year (x 12):

How often do you catch yourself wishing that you could have that car, buy those clothes, or go on that dream holiday.

Just a £5 increase on your average bill, with 30 clients a week, at 30% commission is worth about £35 a week to you, after tax. That is about £1,700 a year. Add that to what you would spend on a holiday anyway, and there is your dream holiday!

YOUR DREAM HOLIDAY - CAR - SHOPPING SPREE ETC.

£5 increase on your average bill x
the amount of clients you do a week:

Ask your salon owner how much more
you would get per week based on your
commission structure and tax rate:

Times this by 12 (if you are paid monthly):

STOP DREAMING
DO SOMETHING AND MAKE IT HAPPEN

It's all about focus. Be brave and set your focus high - you will surprise yourself. I was recently holding a seminar where I asked the audience to set some goals. As I picked people randomly to tell me what their goal was, one person blew me away.

He was a stylist and he wanted to take £5000 per week. That wasn't what impressed me so much; I know what a focused, hardworking stylist can start to take.

No, what impressed me, was when I asked him what he was taking now - "£4,000" was the answer.

You see most people I know, if they were taking £4,000 a week, would probably have an attitude of "I don't need to do any more". But not this guy, he was still reaching for the stars.

We are talking about being 'alive inside' here.

It is a proven fact that having a goal motivates you. The more exciting the goal is, the more motivated you are. Therefore, the first step is to make sure your goals are exciting, as we have just discussed. But sometimes an exciting goal can be scary, and then become de-motivating.

I use a technique called objective mapping, (which has been developed from Tony Buzan's fantastic 'Mind Mapping' concept) to break a goal into achievable chunks, without losing sight of the overall objective.

OBJECTIVE MAPPING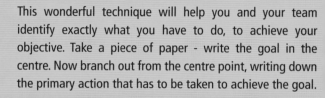

This wonderful technique will help you and your team identify exactly what you have to do, to achieve your objective. Take a piece of paper - write the goal in the centre. Now branch out from the centre point, writing down the primary action that has to be taken to achieve the goal.

Now identify exactly what has to be done to achieve those primary actions. Branch out again by adding the secondary actions for each primary action, before finally identifying when those things need to be done by, and prioritising your plan.

For example - if you want to achieve a higher average bill for yourself, one of the primary goals would be to increase your colour sales. Some of the secondary actions needed to achieve that, could be - learn more about colour, develop a colour menu of quick techniques that you can use for your clients, set yourself a goal of 'x' colours a day, organise a colour evening for your clients - etc.

What this great technique does, is allow you to put a 'goal to fly' in the centre, and then break it down in to do-able chunks around the edge of the map. Start doing those smaller things and you will quickly find yourself heading towards the centre and achieving results that may surprise you.

However, this will not be enough on its' own. Now use the power of your mind as an actor would, to take your performance to a new level.

We talked about changing movies in chapter 7, but here I want to look at making movies - mind movies!

Take your goal, the one in the centre of the objective map and now see yourself having achieved it in your imagination. Create your own mind movie.

Now start to direct it. Make it more powerful. Remember we are talking about being alive inside here. Keep manipulating the movie until you really start to notice your motivation levels increase.

Are you watching yourself as though you are at the movies watching it on screen, or are you in the movie with everything happening around you. You will always be more motivated when you are what is called 'associated' - inside the movie, rather than just watching it.

What about the colours, brightness, size? What can you change to make it more exciting in your mind? Are there phrases or words that would motivate you to achieve this goal - then add them in.

Finally use music, either in your head or in the real world, but if you now add some motivating music to this movie, it will do the trick.

Remember DOGASHI, just do it. All you are doing is what any self respecting sports person or entertainer would do to push their motivation and energy up to the level they need, to perform at the highest standard.

Now whenever you need to increase your motivation to achieve your goal, think about the movie. Make the adjustments you need to amplify it, enjoy it, get excited by it, get 'alive inside' and then use that motivation to get on and do it!

"Be alive inside – smiling from the inside out"

Motivation and energy comes from you, not from other people

choose 3 goals from this chapter that you can take immediate action on:

the fantastic hairdresser
is always
learning

"Excellence is a Journey Not a Destination"

I hope that you remember this from earlier in the book.

It's a quote I have used for years now. It is so important to me; it applies to everything in my life, my work, my relationships, and my knowledge. It doesn't matter who you are, what you know, what you have achieved, however much experience you have, there is always more to learn.

Think about some of the people that you know. Think about great achievers in the world, whether they be to do with politics, world issues, or even sport and entertainment.

What about Kylie, or Madonna? What is it about these people, that enables them to stay at the top when others have fallen. Is it about pure talent? Well I'm not going to make comment here, but I think even they themselves would concede that they do not necessarily have the most gifted voices in the world of entertainment. Their talent is actually one of constant development, learning and change.

Now think about people you know, who are constantly struggling with change. Stressed, under achievers that are constantly under pressure - because they are just not up to what it is they are trying to do.

Whether you like it or not, we live in a world of rapid change today, and if you are not changing with it, you are finished. You just can't stand still any more.

I always liken this to standing next to an ocean, with the 'waves of change' crashing on to the beach. Well we all have a simple choice in our life. We can stand there, feet firmly planted in the sand, arms folded saying "Well I'm not moving, I've always done it like this, why should I change?"

What's going to happen - you are going to get wet feet, because the waves aren't going to stop crashing in.

If you still stand there ignoring the water around your ankles, then eventually, you will be in it up to your knees, and if you still don't move - YOU WILL DROWN!

Look at how many people this is happening to today, look at how many companies don't seem to realise this simple truth.

Think about the retail store, or restaurant that was 'the place to go', but has just become one of the crowd now because they rested on their laurels, they did not keep moving, growing, creating and developing.

If this is hitting home with you, whether it is in your business or personal life, then please go back to the first chapter and go through the Total Life Concept again. This is the only way to help you stay ahead of the game - ride the waves, rather than standing there drowning.

Excellence is a journey not a destination - you don't reach it one day, it's ongoing - it's about constantly, consistently learning.

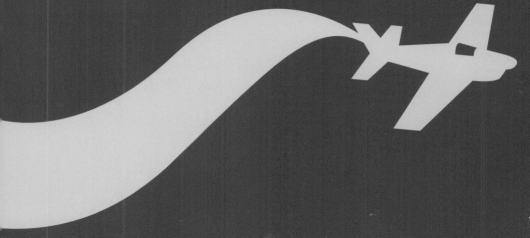

So it's very simple - the world we live in is changing rapidly, which simply means that you have to be consistently, constantly, learning new things. It's like upgrading your computer every two years, but not the software. Still trying to use the programs you were using 5-10 years ago. It just doesn't work.

There are no excuses today either. The availability of information from books, TV, the internet etc., is endless, and easily accessible. However, you do need some sort of structure, otherwise the choice is too great.

HOW YOUR BRAIN LEARNS

Our senses are being bombarded by massive amounts of information in any one moment. The human eye can distinguish 1 photon of light. Our nose can identify one molecule of smell. So much of this is happening at an unconscious level where we are completely unaware of it.

With this level of information entering the brain constantly, we need to have some sort of filter system, which decides what our conscious mind needs to be aware of. Otherwise we would all go insane from the overload.

This filter is what makes focus and goals so important. When you set a goal, you are giving the filter in your brain information that will help it sort through the mass, to make sure that you get what you need.

Imagine going into a reference library, or onto an internet search engine to just 'learn'.

Where on earth would you start?

SET LEARNING GOALS

The learning process starts by establishing your learning focus. As I have already said: "How can you decide how to get somewhere if you don't know where you are going?"

What specifically do you need or want to learn? Now you can start your research. Deciding; how I am going to learn what I need? Will it be from a book? If so which? Or a course. Maybe I can get what I need from the Internet.

I always start each year with a learning focus - What do I want to learn about, this year? At this stage it's not that specific, but I am starting the process. I normally have two focuses, one is to do with my work, my business. The other is to do with me as an individual, in my life generally. I am then able to set a more specific focus for my learning.

15 MINUTES A DAY TO CHANGE YOUR LIFE

Break your learning into small chunks. It is not possible to concentrate properly for much longer than about 15 -20 minutes. It is also a fact that we always remember more from the beginning, and the end, of a learning session. So if you read for an hour, you have one beginning, one end, and one huge middle that you will find difficult to recall.

Read for 4 x 15 minute sessions and not only will your concentration be better, but you will also have 4 beginnings and 4 ends.

I always felt I should read more, learn more, but I got bored with learning books and rarely finished them. I also always had the excuse that so many people give me - "I don't have time to read".

So I set myself a goal 17 years ago, to read a learning book for a minimum of 15 minutes a day. I stuck to it religiously. Fifteen minutes worth of learning a day is a minimum of 90 hours a year. That's a lot of learning for someone who had no time. Anybody can find 15 minutes a day. Try it. It will change the level of information you take onboard dramatically.

Project forward 10 years and think about the impact a minimum of 900 hours focused learning would have on you and your life.

the fantastic hairdresser
minds their own business

So what is that we should be learning? Well of course, some of it is obvious, although to be honest it doesn't always seem so. Too many stylists seem to think that having qualified there is nothing more to learn. Trainees - who miss the opportunity to learn valuable information that will literally affect the rest of their life, because they duck into the staff room for a quick cigarette.

However, if you are going to be a fantastic hairdresser, then there are a few things that you need to do. I suggest that you have a personal development plan. Let's start that here.

You should incorporate four areas into your plan.

1. The core skills you need to do your job to the highest level - cutting, colour, hair up etc.

2. The other stuff - the things you realise from this book that you need to develop to achieve your goals, creativity, communication skills etc.

3. The business - understanding your industry, how it works, current news and issues, who the major players are, etc.

4. Your future prospects - what are your goals? Do you want to be a manager one day? Do you want to be in the art team, or a trainer? Now start to identify what you can do to prepare for that happening one day.

For now just choose one thing from each area. For example in the core skills part of your plan, you might get booked on to a specific course. Maybe you decide to improve your colour knowledge.

In section 2, you could start to work on your communication skills, by reading a book on body language and attending one of the Fantastic Hairdresser seminars.

You could make a commitment to reading the Hairdressers Journal properly every week. To learn more about the industry, and finally begin to take more of an interest in the management side of the business - maybe asking for some small extra responsibilities to get you going.

Now use the objective mapping tool, and draw up your personal development plan for the year. Make it creative, use pictures and colour. Add a mind movie of how you will be when you have completed the plan.

Start by thinking about what you are going to do to develop yourself in each of those four areas, and then do it. Do this every year. But start now. Use this chapters' action page to draw up a development plan for yourself.

Go back through the book and look at the action pages. You should have written down some of the areas that you know you have to develop, to grow, in order to achieve your goals. Now incorporate those into your plan on the action page for this chapter, and you are on your way.

All you have to do now is make it happen!

Do this regularly and over a period of time, you will quickly become one of the best, A FANTASTIC HAIRDRESSER

THE FANTASTIC HAIRDRESSER IS STILL LEARNING

"Learning is the first step, not the last"

It's the action you take with what you learn that makes the difference

SUCCESS

Your personal development plan:

Finally, I have added one thing to the 7 characteristics of a fantastic hairdresser - they have fun!

It is always my sign off. I didn't realise it until someone pointed it out to me. You know how some people always say; "see ya" when they leave you, or "take care". It's just a habit, and as this friend pointed out to me, mine is "have fun". I didn't realise I was saying it, but I love it. It sums me up more than anything else I could say.

I have always believed that if you are not having fun - what's the point! Anybody who is fantastic at what they do, must be having fun. It's a cycle - you have to be having fun in order to be fantastic, and if you are being fantastic - you are having fun. We normally talk about breaking out of a cycle, but not this one. What a great way to spend your life!

The fantastic hairdresser is having fun, and this is why:

They have passion; they always remember why they became a hairdresser, and what they love about it. They understand that they do a worthwhile job. That what they do has a real impact on people. They always remember how lucky they are to have the freedom to do a job that is creative, fun, and motivating.

They know that it's delight the client wants - not service, and that they have to be aware of the little things that can lose them their clients - it's not the lions that bite you - it's the gnats. They also understand that it's not enough to just do it right - you have to do it right consistently to earn the trust that will grow your column.

They inspire people - their clients, their team - their audience; by understanding people, really getting to know them, and what makes them tick. Learning about them by asking good questions and then listening with their eyes and ears before motivating them with positive communication.

They are an ambassador for their salon, their industry, and themselves. They realise that hairdressing is a business - a creative business - but a business that has to be profitable or there is no job. They know they need help, that everyone in the team has a value and can help them to achieve their goals. They have high personal values and standards of behaviour that ensure their ultimate success.

They are performers - they are on stage the moment they step on to the salon floor. They have the skills and knowledge to give them confidence, the understanding that their fears are only in their mind, and that they can change those movies and take control.

They are alive inside - motivated from the inside out! Knowing precisely where they are going. Understanding that the only limits they have are the limits they put on themselves, and making their own movies to motivate themselves to take action.

Finally, they are **always, always learning**. They understand that excellence is a journey, not a destination. They know how they learn, and how to create a personal development plan - to gain the skills and information they need to be the best!

That's why they are having fun!!

It's time for you now. Time for you to have the fun that becoming a fantastic hairdresser will give you. I am going to finish this book the same way I finish every seminar I ever do with a question for you. A question that cuts straight to the heart of everything we have discussed in this book.

But first a couple of other things that are important to me. I hope you have enjoyed this book. It has been so exciting writing it, I just couldn't wait to get it into your hands. I really hope that you have enjoyed reading it as much as I have writing it.

Secondly, I hope that you have found it worthwhile and that as you have been going through, there have been things that made you think - Think about yourself, your clients, your salon, and our industry. Maybe I will see you on one of our seminars in the near future so that you can learn even more about what makes a Fantastic Hairdresser.

So, if you have enjoyed this book - great, if you have found it worthwhile - even better, but my last question to you is quite simply... **WHAT ARE YOU GOING TO DO ABOUT IT?**

Take the information inside these pages and make it a blueprint for your future.

IF YOU WANT CHANGE - CHANGE SOMETHING!

Have fun, Alan

Want to know more about what else we can do for you and your business?

For details on 'The Fantastic Hairdresser' seminar series, further company information and other courses for both the U.K. and Internationally please go to: www.fantastic-hairdresser.co.uk

The Fantastic Hairdresser Company
Barley Mow Centre,
10 Barley Mow Passage,
Chiswick,
W4 4PH

+44 (0) 20 8 996 1644
info@fantastic-hairdresser.co.uk

Other contact information:

Book design by:
bluw□□□
Thornton House
Thornton Rd
Wimbledon
SW19 4NG

+44 (0) 20 8 405 6406
www.bluw.co.uk

Alan has never been one to 'sit still' when it comes to learning, achieving and growing.

Every time in his career, whether it was as a hairdresser or in what he does now, when a goal is reached, he always has the drive and desire to go further.

He'll tell you he thrives on challenge!

As you know, when you are passionate about something, you take on a whole different persona. It 'fires you up' inside. Because of Alan's long standing relationship with the hairdressing industry, his passion for its success and the people who work within it, he is highly motivated to share his knowledge and experience.

Alan is an excellent communicator. He has been standing in front of audiences for over 20 years and has inspired many. His work is acknowledged in the U.K., as being hugely influential on the development of the hairdressing business.

His ultimate aim is to spread his philosophy of: "Making the most of your life, achieving the successes you desire and having fun doing it".